HOLISTIC
SELF-CARE
GUIDED
JOURNAL

HOLISTIC SELF-CARE GUIDED JOURNAL

NURTURE Yourself
EXPAND Your Mind
EMBRACE Who You Are

CARLEY SCHWEET

ROCKRIDGE
PRESS

For general information on our other products and services or to obtain technical sup-port, please contact our Customer Care Department within the United States at (866) 744-2665, or outside the United States at (510) 253-0500.

Rockridge Press publishes its books in a variety of electronic and print formats. Some content that appears in print may not be available in electronic books, and vice versa.

Interior & Cover Designer: Karmen Lizzul
Art Producer: Samantha Ulban
Editor: Emily Angell
Production Editor: Rachel Taenzler
All images courtesy of © iStock/Svetlana Zybina.
Author photo courtesy of © Ryan Flynn Photography.

ISBN: Print 978-1-64611-792-5
RO

THIS JOURNAL BELONGS TO

_____

"AN EMPTY LANTERN
PROVIDES NO LIGHT.
SELF-CARE IS THE FUEL
THAT ALLOWS YOUR LIGHT
TO SHINE BRIGHTLY."

—Unknown

CONTENTS

INTRODUCTION

Self-care has the power to transform and reshape your life. I know because I've experienced its power firsthand.

I'm Carley, a recovering people-pleaser. I lived most of my life helping others before considering myself or addressing my needs for happiness. This habitual behavior left me burned-out, overwhelmed, and unfulfilled in many areas of my life, especially in my job and personal relationships.

Part of me believed that I had to first prove myself as a "good person" in order to tend to my requirements for a happy life. The truth is I had lost touch with my needs for happiness long ago. I instead temporarily fueled myself by soaking up the demands and wants of those around me. I chalked up my overwhelming stress and sleepless nights to the belief that I wasn't trying hard enough. Day in and day out, I continued to lose my true self deeper into what I believed was the service of others.

In the early stages of my self-care journey, I discovered the power of journaling. Sitting down and connecting with my thoughts and feelings in an approachable way helped me mold a new, supportive relationship with myself. This small but impactful act was unlike anything I had never done before.

Self-care helped me rediscover my voice, and quickly, I realized she had a lot to say. I had been ignoring her for far too long.

Today, I am a self-care coach and author of *Boundaries with Soul* and the journal you hold in your hands.

My work focuses on helping others to leverage their own power of self-care to move closer to a life that includes a sense of joy, empowerment, and self-assuredness to help them rediscover and reclaim their voice.

It's essential to acknowledge that self-care isn't just about self-indulgence. Instead, self-care is a profoundly personal and holistic practice that addresses all the parts of your being. It involves working to reshape your mind-set, grow your self-worth, and redefine your relationship with yourself. Self-care goes beyond the physical and deep into the emotional, allowing you to get back in touch with who you are and to get what you most desire out of your life. It also opens your eyes to the realization that what you previously desired is not necessarily what makes you happiest.

This journal contains tools to support you on this transformative journey. Tucked inside these pages, you'll find inspiring prompts, thought-provoking exercises, positive affirmations, and powerful quotes. All of these elements are designed to help guide you through the process of creating your unique holistic self-care practice.

Please note that while journaling is an excellent way to work through emotions, any ongoing feelings of anxiety and depression should be addressed by a medical professional. This book is not a replacement for a therapist, medication, or medical treatment, and there is no shame in seeking help. Reaching out for support is a powerful act of self-care and something you deserve to access if needed.

Whether you, like me, are a people-pleaser or you just seek a greater sense of self-worth, authenticity, or joy in your life, I welcome you to use this journal to help create transformational self-care practices. These prompts and exercises are designed to transform the way you think and do things. You'll see how even the simplest practices can shape your future and move you closer to the life you're worthy of living, simply by being you.

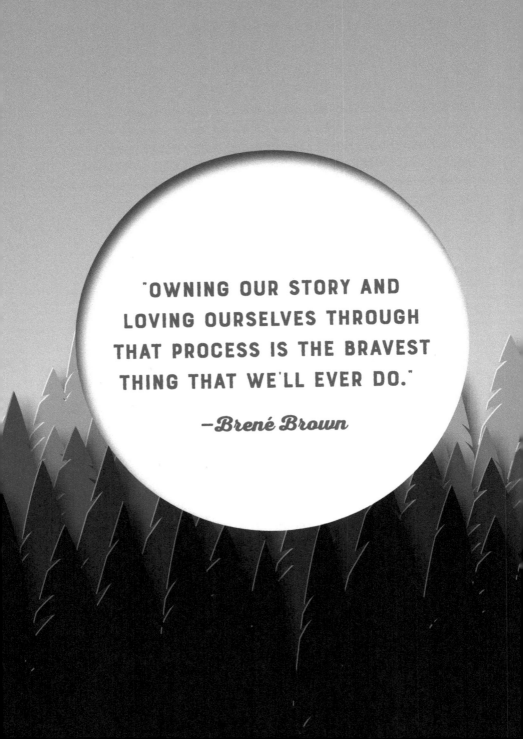

"OWNING OUR STORY AND LOVING OURSELVES THROUGH THAT PROCESS IS THE BRAVEST THING THAT WE'LL EVER DO."

—Brené Brown

Section One

NURTURE
YOURSELF

nur · ture: to care for and
encourage growth
or development

We all have a story. A unique path that led us to become who we are today. Every journey is filled with twists and turns, which can sometimes cause us to lose sight of who we are and what we desire most in our lives.

Getting back in touch with yourself can feel like a daunting task. You may ask, *Who am I, anyway?* But the process starts with one small but powerful word: *nurture*.

By nurturing yourself from the inside out, you'll gain self-awareness and, with that, precious insight into the thoughts and emotions you experience regularly but may be overlooking.

With this information, you can begin to build a solid foundation for self-acceptance and your holistic self-care practice. This practice will spark the courage to care for yourself, create a newfound sense of resilience, and guide you on the path to positive change.

REDISCOVER THE POWER
OF NURTURE

Reconnect with what it feels like to be nurtured. Write about a memory—big or small—of a time you felt supported by someone else.

_____

_____

_____

_____

Pay attention to what that nurturing made you feel and how you felt about the other person. Did you admire their compassion, patience, or loving heart? Or did you simply feel buoyed by their steady encouragement?

_____

_____

_____

_____

Now, consider the feelings that come from being nurtured by someone else. How can you apply those feelings to yourself and your new self-care practice?

_____

_____

_____

_____

HOLISTIC LIFE ASSESSMENT: PART ONE

Let's take a deeper look at the overall health of different sections in your life. Use the circle shown or grab a blank piece of paper and pen and draw a circle divided into six sections. Label each section as follows.

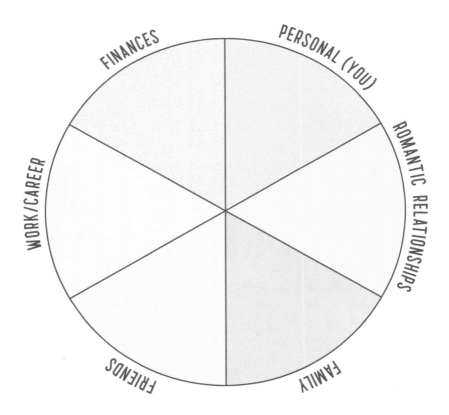

Decide where to place a dot in each of the segments. The closer the dot is to the outside of the circle, the stronger you feel about the overall health of that area. Connect all the dots with straight lines and assess. Are you surprised by your results?

_____

_____

_____

_____

_____

This exercise is designed to show you where you can begin to make changes in the way you care for yourself. Write a few sentences about what you discovered and how you can begin to nurture yourself more effectively where you need it most.

_____

_____

_____

_____

_____

_____

_____

_____

_____

_____

_____

WHAT DOES NURTURING FEEL LIKE?

Circle the words that describe what *nurturing* feels like to you.

Supportive	Courageous
Gentle	Loving
Brave	Compassionate
Kind	Encouraging
Honest	Safe

Make a list of your own words or thoughts here.

_____

_____

_____

_____

_____

_____

_____

_____

_____

_____

HI, SELF. IT'S ME!

Getting back in touch with your innermost thoughts and feelings may require a reintroduction of yourself—to yourself. Fill in the blanks in the following prompt.

Dear _____,

YOUR NAME HERE

It's me, _____,

YOUR NAME HERE

Remember? The person who loves to _____ and really enjoys _____.

Lately, I've been feeling a little _____, so I'm creating holistic self-care practices in hopes of _____. To be honest, _____, I'm most excited about how this

YOUR NAME HERE

practice can help me _____.

Above all, it's my desire to care better for myself that brought me here. I'm ready to nurture my mind, body, and soul and feel _____ while doing so.

Love,

_____

YOUR NAME HERE

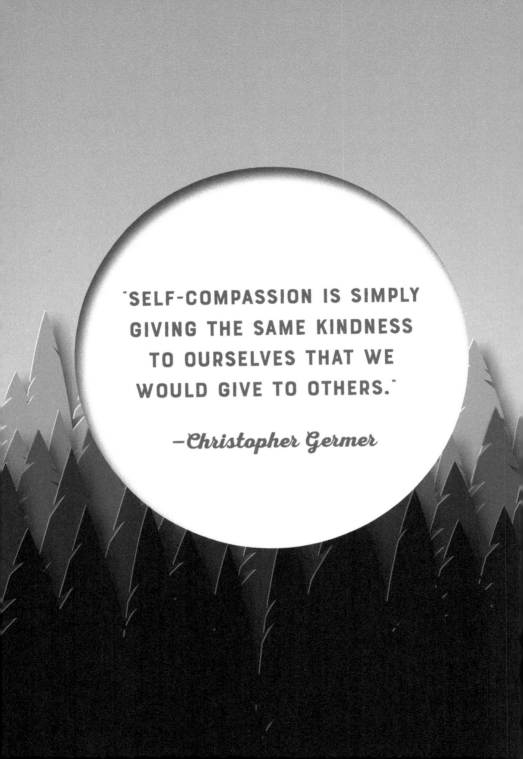

"SELF-COMPASSION IS SIMPLY
GIVING THE SAME KINDNESS
TO OURSELVES THAT WE
WOULD GIVE TO OTHERS."

—Christopher Germer

FEELINGS BAROMETER

Take stock of your feelings! This process can help you gain precious insight into what brings joy—and, conversely, stress—into your life. Answer the following questions to help you tune into your current behaviors surrounding different parts of your life.

I feel most like myself when I'm _____

_____

When doing this, I feel _____

_____

I find myself most overwhelmed or stressed when _____

_____

When I feel overwhelmed, I tend to _____

_____

To help me move away from feeling stressed, I'd like to start

_____ *in hopes of feeling more*

_____

AN AFFIRMATION FOR NURTURING YOURSELF

Affirmations can help solidify a thought or mind-set you'd like to regard as true. The more you repeat an affirmation, the stronger your belief around that statement becomes. Repeat the following affirmation aloud three times.

I AM WORKING ON NURTURING THOSE PARTS OF ME THAT REQUIRE UNCONDITIONAL LOVE, HEALING, AND ENCOURAGEMENT.

STREAM OF CONSCIOUSNESS JOURNALING

Stream of consciousness journaling simply means putting your thoughts and ideas onto paper as they come, without hesitation or judgment. Use the space provided to let your thoughts flow out of your mind and into the world. Don't stop for spelling and grammar mistakes—just let your subconscious mind take over your writing hand. If you need help getting started, answer the following question.

I was drawn to this journal because . . .

_____

_____

_____

_____

_____

_____

_____

_____

_____

_____

_____

_____

_____

_____

CREATE A PRESENT MOMENT FOR YOURSELF

Brew a mug of your favorite tea and take a break from the digital world.

As you sip, leave your phone facedown and focus on whatever thoughts or feelings come to mind. This activity may feel uncomfortable at first. Be gentle and give yourself time to decompress and adjust.

This is a great self-care exercise to make a habit of. Tune out the outside noise and take time to simply be in your thoughts several times a day if you wish.

AFFIRMATIONS FROM WITHIN

Often, we rely on others to encourage and nurture us to feel validated. In reality, self-care will empower you to create those feelings on your own.

Write three sentences other people have said to you that made you feel good.

1. _____

_____

2. _____

_____

3. _____

_____

Now, look within and write three affirmations inspired by your favorite qualities about yourself. For an example of an affirmation, look back at page 10.

1. _____

_____

2. _____

_____

3. _____

_____

Revisit these affirmations often.

TURN INWARD: A
BREATHING EXERCISE

▸ Close your eyes, and place your hands on your stomach.

▸ Take three deep breaths, in through your nose and out through your mouth.

▸ Repeat with your hands on your heart and then on your throat.

▸ Then return your hands to where you felt the most uncomfortable breathing into.

▸ Breathe into that spot for five breaths.

▸ Notice how the internal tension begins to loosen with each supportive breath? Call on this practice whenever needed during your journey.

WAYS TO NURTURE YOURSELF

Create a go-to list of three simple ways you can care for yourself when you need to decompress. Feel free to add to this list over time.

Turn to this page when you're feeling stressed or overwhelmed, and pick the activity that feels the most supportive for you in the moment.

WHAT YOU ADMIRE MOST

Write down five *nonphysical* qualities you admire about yourself.
Explain why they are so special to you—it's okay to brag!

1. _____

_____

_____

2. _____

_____

_____

3. _____

_____

_____

4. _____

_____

_____

5. _____

_____

_____

FOOD FOR THE SOUL

Prepare your favorite meal for yourself (and a loved one, if you wish). If you're up for it, try preparing something completely new and tap into your creativity.

While eating your special meal, focus on slowing down and enjoying each bite. Feel how nurturing the simple act of eating can be.

HOLISTIC LIFE ASSESSMENT: PART TWO

Do you remember the holistic life assessment you did earlier (page 4)? Flip to that page and take a look. Now, answer the following questions with the six categories in mind: personal (yourself), romantic relationships, family, friends, work/career, finances.

The area that brings me the most joy in my life is

_____

_____

The area that empowers me the most is

_____

_____

The area that inspires me the most is

_____

_____

The area that leaves me feeling nurtured is

_____

_____

If you don't have your assessment handy, feel free to repeat that exercise on a blank piece of paper.

AFFIRMATIONS FOR EMPOWERMENT

Write down three affirmations that empower you by boosting your mental and emotional well-being. For example, *I am creating my own happiness by prioritizing my well-being.*

1. _____

_____

_____

_____

2. _____

_____

_____

_____

3. _____

_____

_____

_____

"YOUR JOB IS TO FILL
UP YOUR OWN CUP SO
IT OVERFLOWS. THEN, YOU
CAN JOYFULLY SERVE OTHERS
FROM YOUR SAUCER."

— *Lisa Nichols*

GET AHEAD WITH A PLAN

An important part of self-care is acknowledging uncomfortable emotions. Now that you're more in touch with your mental and emotional state, create a supportive game plan based on the following scenarios.

When I feel overwhelmed, I will _____

_____

_____

When I feel stressed, I will _____

_____

_____

When I feel burned-out, I will _____

_____

_____

When I feel ignored, I will _____

_____

_____

Add your own game plan here. _____

_____

_____

A MEDITATION FOR SELF-LOVE

▸ Sit in a chair with your feet flat on the ground. Set a timer for three minutes if you wish.

▸ Rest your hands on your legs with palms facing up and gently close your eyes.

▸ Calm your mind and take three deep breaths, in through your nose and out through your mouth.

▸ Continue the breathing pattern.

▸ With each inhalation, silently repeat the words *I accept myself as I am.*

▸ With each exhalation, silently repeat the words *I release self-judgment.*

▸ When time is up, gently open your eyes.

YOUR RECIPE FOR SELF-CARE

Self-care is a unique practice that varies from person to person. To embrace the idea of what it looks like for you, create your unique recipe for self-care using the following word bank.

Qualities: patience, grace, forgiveness, compassion, reflection, love, mindfulness, awareness, courage

Measurements: a pinch, a teaspoon, a tablespoon, a dash, a cup, a handful, a gallon, a heap

Here is a sample recipe:
 A pinch of courage
 A handful of patience
 A cup of compassion
 A heap of love

Mix thoroughly and use as needed. When combined, these ingredients will provide what you need to begin to create a foundational self-care practice.

Now write your personal recipe for self-care.

"IN ANY GIVEN MOMENT
WE HAVE TWO OPTIONS: TO
STEP FORWARD INTO GROWTH
OR STEP BACK INTO SAFETY."

—*Abraham Maslow*

Section Two

EXPAND
YOUR MIND

---

ex · pand: to open up, unfold

Now that you've reconnected with your thoughts and examined some personal feelings, it's time to focus on shifting to a more positive mind-set.

Creating new practices of any kind requires you to shed your old way of thinking. It calls on you to look at your life with a more expansive lens and a fresh perspective. By shifting your mind-set, you can feel better about things you may have previously been hung up on, become empowered with the possibilities for growth, and care for yourself more impactfully than ever before.

Admittedly, it takes courage to intentionally choose to shift your current way of thinking and the behavior that follows. Give yourself the chance to practice, and be patient with yourself.

FACE CHANGE WITH COURAGE

Growing and expanding your mind-set takes courage, but the benefits are worth the effort. Use the space provided to write a list of your current fears around growth or change.

By declaring your fears on paper, you will actually make them feel more approachable.

AN AFFIRMATION FOR GROWTH

Sit in a quiet place without any distractions, and repeat the following affirmation out loud three times. Spend a few moments thinking about how your energy shifted after repeating the affirmation.

I GIVE MYSELF SPACE
TO LEARN HOW TO DO THINGS
IN A NEW WAY.

SHED OLD MIND-SETS

A mind-set I'd like to release that no longer serves me is _____

_____

_____

_____

_____

_____

_____

I'd like to shed this mind-set because _____

_____

_____

_____

_____

_____

_____

_____

_____

_____

_____

A new mind-set I'd like to replace it with is _____

_____

_____

_____

_____

CLEAR SPACE FOR CHANGE

Working to expand your mind-set can feel intimidating. You might find yourself being judgmental of the changes you wish to make.

To combat this self-criticism, talk to yourself like you would a friend and list three benefits you could experience by doing everyday things with a different mind-set. If you're up to it, list a few action items that will help you create these shifts in your life.

"THE HAPPINESS OF YOUR
LIFE DEPENDS ON THE QUALITY
OF YOUR THOUGHTS."

—*Marcus Aurelius*

ENVISION YOUR
FEARLESS FUTURE

What does your future look like if you have no fear? As you write, encourage yourself to dream expansively and know that *nothing* is off-limits or out of reach.

_____

_____

_____

_____

_____

_____

_____

_____

_____

_____

_____

_____

_____

_____

_____

_____

_____

_____

_____

SAY "NO" IN ORDER TO GROW

Setting boundaries and denying requests that don't serve you can help you reclaim your precious time and energy. Write out three commitments or requests that you'd like to start saying "no" to instead of your usual "yes." Then, next to each, write what you will gain (time, energy, money, etc.) by opting for "no" over "yes."

SAY NO TO...	GAIN
1.	
2.	
3.	

EMBRACE THE POWER
OF BOUNDARIES

Keep in mind the benefits you listed in the previous exercise as you work through this activity.

Expand outside your comfort zone and say "no" in real life to three things, big or small, that you'd usually say "yes" to, such as a request for your time that causes more stress than happiness or a social gathering that doesn't light you up inside.

Notice the changes or feelings that occur with each decision.

SHIFT YOUR THOUGHT PATTERNS

A shift in thinking can generate a ripple effect in your life. The expansion into a new thought process can positively impact everything you currently know. What are some current thought patterns you'd like to change? List three. If you wish, explain why each is important to you.

MIND-OPENING MEDITATION

It can be hard to find a moment of silence in our busy lives, but this exercise challenges you to create an intentional 60 seconds of calm and stillness in your day.

▸ When you're ready, sit on the floor or in a chair, and gently close your eyes.

▸ Focus on your breath, and expand beyond the current thoughts in your mind and into a place of calm. Leave all judgment behind. If you get distracted, come back to your breath.

▸ When time is up, gently open your eyes. Congratulations—you just meditated!

WHERE WILL LOVE TAKE YOU?

Grow your mind-set by expanding your love. Imagine how transformational it would feel to think and speak positively about yourself and others while leaving negative thought patterns behind.

   With this mind-set shift in all areas of your life, what concrete changes could you anticipate occurring?

PUT A POSITIVE
SPIN ON THINGS

Take notice of how many times you use the
word "sorry" throughout your day. Do you
reserve it for times you're genuinely sorry?

Many people use "sorry" as a filler
word, unsure what to say in its place. Try
practicing gratitude instead of apologizing.
This way, "Sorry I'm late" becomes "Thanks
for being so patient!"

Give this practice a try and note how
you feel.

CREATE YOUR GROWTH MIND-SET

Rewrite the following three sentences to signify a growth mind-set.

1. **When you think this:** *If I'm not perfect, I'm not good enough.*
    Try this instead:

    _____

    _____

    _____

2. **When you think this:** *I'm being selfish by communicating my wants and needs.*
    Try this instead:

    _____

    _____

    _____

3. **When you think this:** *I don't know enough about (enter subject here) to succeed at it.*
    Try this instead:

    _____

    _____

    _____

CHOOSE YOUR WORDS WISELY

Starting conversations with the words "I feel" instead of blaming others with "You" can be transformational in your relationships and can allow you to focus more on what you're feeling than on what you believe the other person did.

How would integrating the words "I feel" transform and expand your conversations? Write a few sentences that might help you shift into a more positive dialogue.

"THE GREATEST
DISCOVERY OF ALL TIME
IS THAT A PERSON CAN
CHANGE HIS FUTURE BY MERELY
CHANGING HIS ATTITUDE."

—*Oprah Winfrey*

WHAT DOES SELF-CARE
MEAN TO YOU NOW?

Now that we've explored the deeper meaning of self-care, write a few sentences about your updated definition of self-care.

NOTICE IN OTHERS,
NOTICE IN YOURSELF

Sometimes, what irritates us about others reflects what we need to work on in ourselves.

Take some time to write down behaviors of others that you find frustrating, and reflect on whether you possess any of these qualities.

_____

_____

_____

_____

_____

_____

Write down three actions you could take to expand your current mind-set around the traits you carry, and work to seek patience with yourself. Accept and be kind to yourself through this process.

_____

_____

_____

_____

_____

_____

_____

_____

AN AFFIRMATION FOR GROWTH

Take three deep breaths, and then repeat the following affirmation:

I TRUST THAT WHEN THE GROWTH PROCESS IS UNCOMFORTABLE, THERE'S A LESSON FOR ME TO LEARN. I WILL SEEK TO EMBRACE THE LESSON.

Take a few minutes to think about what this message means to you.

WRITE DOWN YOUR INTENTIONS

Now that you've explored the idea of expanding your mind-set, write a handful of intentions around how you will work to experience the world in a new way.

EXPAND YOUR MIND-SET

Throughout this section, you've been presented with opportunities to expand your mind-set and create growth. List three additional ways that you can broaden your way of thinking to create positive change in your life.

1. _____
_____
_____
_____
_____
_____

2. _____
_____
_____
_____
_____
_____

3. _____
_____
_____
_____
_____

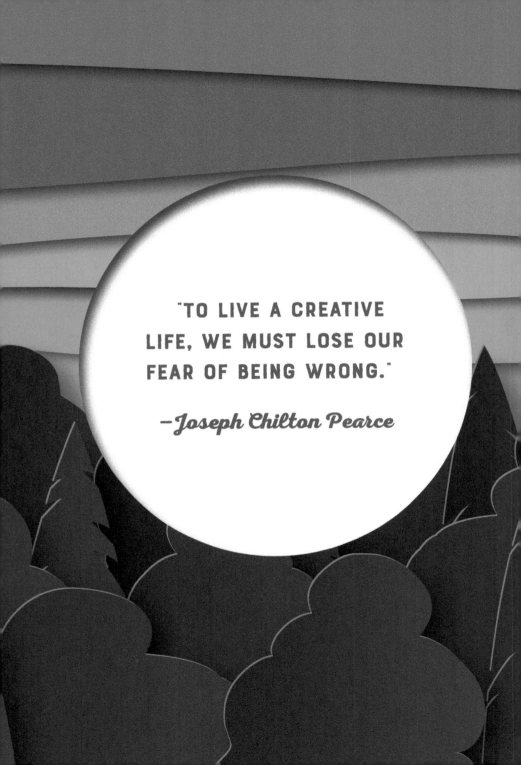

"TO LIVE A CREATIVE LIFE, WE MUST LOSE OUR FEAR OF BEING WRONG."

—Joseph Chilton Pearce

Section Three

GET CREATIVE

cre · a · tiv · i · ty: the use of imagination or original ideas

Creativity is a powerful tool. It can inspire you to step outside your comfort zone and discover different ways to "fill your cup." By embracing creativity, you're bound to find new forms of peace and joy within your life while reconnecting to your youthful playfulness.

Creativity is much more than a fun way to express yourself. Studies have shown that embracing creativity can provide an inspiring boost of energy that can help you feel more enthusiastic about your life.

You don't need to be an artist or an excellent writer to be creative. In fact, to live a creative life, it's important to embrace the fact that perfection doesn't exist. The more you surrender to embracing your imperfect and artistic nature, the more inspired and fearless you'll begin to feel.

This process requires a little self-assurance, a fresh perspective, and an increased sense of awareness—all of which you've been working to develop.

As you work through this section, focus on surrendering to the process and releasing self-judgment. Your creative instincts are ready and waiting.

REDISCOVER YOUR INNER CHILD

First, let's reconnect you with your innate sense of playfulness—
it's there, I promise! Answer the following questions to help you
rediscover your playful side.

As a kid, in my free time, I loved to

Something that brought me immense feelings of joy was

I felt so carefree when

CHALLENGE YOURSELF

In the blank space provided, write your full name three times with your nondominant hand. Notice how awkward and unnatural it feels? Tapping back into creativity can feel that way if it's been awhile. Nevertheless, keep practicing—it'll get easier!

REDEFINE WHAT CREATIVITY MEANS TO YOU

Creativity can sometimes feel like a box that you don't fit into instantly. It can help to redefine your definition of creativity so expressing yourself feels more approachable.

What does creativity look like to you, for you, as an individual?

YOU'RE ALREADY CREATIVE

Think about your current life. In what ways are you already practicing creativity but not giving yourself creative credit? Some examples include cooking a meal without a recipe, fixing something around your home, and reorganizing a messy space. List a few instances here.

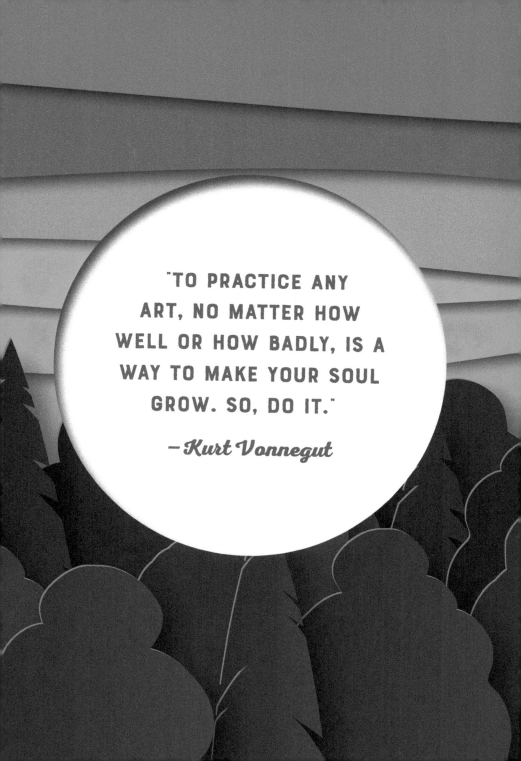

"TO PRACTICE ANY
ART, NO MATTER HOW
WELL OR HOW BADLY, IS A
WAY TO MAKE YOUR SOUL
GROW. SO, DO IT."

— Kurt Vonnegut

AN AFFIRMATION FOR CREATIVITY

Find a quiet space and repeat the following affirmation out loud three times:

I AM CREATIVE IN MY OWN UNIQUE WAY. CREATIVITY HAS THE POWER TO FUEL ME AND BRING JOY AND PEACE BACK INTO MY LIFE.

How does repeating this statement make you feel?

WHAT'S STOPPING YOU?

Sometimes, we don't tap into our creativity because we don't feel imaginative enough to even attempt to create. The limiting beliefs you have about yourself might hold you back from creating something unique and beautiful that brings joy into your life.

In the space below, write down three beliefs you hold about your creativity. For example, *I feel I'm not skilled at drawing, I feel I can't carry a tune, I feel that numbers are more my thing, etc.*

1. _____

_____

_____

_____

2. _____

_____

_____

_____

3. _____

_____

_____

_____

Now, let's confront these beliefs and reaffirm your creativity. One-by-one, read each limiting belief out loud. On the lines below, add the following statement to each limiting belief: *but I am creative in my own ways, and I can't wait to discover more about my unique creativity!*

For example, *I feel I'm not skilled at drawing* becomes *I feel I'm not a skilled drawer, but I am creative in my own ways, and I can't wait to discover more about my unique creativity!*

1. _____

_____

_____

_____

2. _____

_____

_____

_____

3. _____

_____

_____

_____

READY, SET, DRAW!

In the frame provided, express your creativity by creating a self-portrait of yourself at your happiest. (Don't worry if you're a stick figure artist—simple or abstract art is fine, too!)

CREATE CREATIVITY TODAY

There are so many ways that you can be creative, even if you don't believe that you are. Whether you're able to whip up something delicious in the kitchen or find yourself doodling while you're on a phone call, we all have creative potential.

When you think about your life with a holistic mind-set, where do you feel the least creative or inspired?

So, let's boost your creativity! List three creativity-driven activities you do or can do in that area to help fill your creative cup.

1.

2.

3.

See! Look how innately creative you are. If you identified new activities you could do to boost creativity in a specific area, think about trying one of them out and note how it makes you feel.

WHAT INSPIRES YOU?

Find an encouraging quote that speaks to you. Write it in the space provided and try out a new style of handwriting while you're at it. You can try writing it in cursive, calligraphy, backward, extra squiggly—whatever feels fun and fresh to you.

WRITE A SHORT STORY

It's time to tap into your imagination and your memory. Write a short story about an adventure you took as a kid. Aim for at least five sentences.

Now reflect on your story. Put yourself back in the moment. Remember how you felt? Close your eyes and let those feelings fill you up.

TRY SOMETHING NEW

Adventures aren't just for kids—adults need adventure, too! Creative pursuits, especially something new, require a sense of vulnerability. Work to embrace vulnerability by doing something you've never done before: Sign up for a cooking class, make small talk with a stranger, take up dancing lessons, or try yoga for the first time.

Feel yourself step out of your comfort zone and strive to do the same with your creative side. How did it make you feel?

WHAT WOULD YOU DO IF . . . ?

What would you do if nothing was off-limits in your life? No dream or goal is too big, too lofty, or too intimidating. Answer in the space provided and declare your vision to the universe.

WHO MAKES YOU SMILE?

In the space provided, draw someone who brings a smile to your face. When you're finished, write a few sentences explaining why you chose this person.

If you wish, you can carefully rip the page out to share with them or take a photo and send it their way!

"CREATIVITY IS INVENTING, EXPERIMENTING, GROWING, TAKING RISKS, BREAKING RULES, MAKING MISTAKES, AND HAVING FUN."

—Mary Lou Cook

DOODLE AWAY

Like freewriting or stream of consciousness journaling, doodling is a great way to let your mind wander and stimulate the creativity-driven right side of your brain.

Set a timer for three minutes and doodle without expectation in the space provided.

MEDITATION FOR HARNESSING CREATIVITY

▸ Set a timer for three minutes, if you wish, and sit in a quiet space.

▸ Gently close your eyes. Breathe in through your nose and out through your mouth.

▸ As you breathe, visualize yourself in your most uninhibited creative state.

> What are you doing?

> What are you wearing?

> What colors are surrounding you?

> How does your creativity make you feel?

▸ Continue to breathe intentionally while focusing on this vision.

▸ When the time is up, gently open your eyes.

Call on this meditation anytime you need a boost of creativity or wish to tap back into your creative self. Remember, your creative side is always waiting—you simply need to tap back into it as needed!

A LETTER TO YOURSELF

Writing a letter to yourself can help you stay on track with a commitment. Fill in the blanks below.

Dear _____,
YOUR NAME HERE

I'm blown away by how creative I really am!

    It's felt so _____ and _____ to tap

back into my creativity and embrace the imperfections. In

this process, I've found that embracing my creative side

will empower me to _____ and ultimately feel

_____ about myself.

    Moving forward, I commit to _____

at least DAILY / WEEKLY / MONTHLY to help fuel my
CIRCLE ONE

creative side.

Love,

_____
YOUR NAME HERE

ACRONYM ART

You may have done this as a kid, but perhaps with different results. In the space below, write your name in a single vertical line with one letter on each line. Then think of a positive word to describe yourself that starts with the same letter found in your name.

When finished, repeat the words out loud, starting with "I am ..." Don't be afraid to say them out loud—you chose these words!

YOUR NEWLY FOUND CREATIVITY

Set a timer for five minutes if you wish. Freewrite about how your newly discovered creativity will help you fill your own cup and create a new way of caring for yourself.

"DON'T TRY TO RUSH PROGRESS. REMEMBER, A STEP FORWARD, NO MATTER HOW SMALL, IS A STEP IN THE RIGHT DIRECTION."

—Kara Goucher

MOVE YOUR BODY

move · ment: *the act of changing physical location or position*

There's something to be said about the power of physical movement, no matter how big or small.

When you move your body with intention, you are doing more than building physical strength. You're fueling a positive mind-set, producing more energy, and creating a life that feels lighter and more fluid. It's no surprise that being active can help increase your overall health and wellness, but studies show that regular physical activity can also help improve your memory and sharpen your thinking skills.

Movement and exercise are foundational parts of self-care and have the potential to rewire the way we think about ourselves. They are powerful enough to generate positive feelings and allow us to lean into and welcome change, making us more dynamic, adaptable, and grounded.

No matter what physical movement looks like for you, know that you're doing yourself an invaluable service by showing up for this new adventure. So lace up your shoes and let's get moving!

YOUR UNIQUE MOVEMENT

Exercise is a personal experience. An activity that your friend loves might not jibe with you—that's okay! Work on finding activities that feel supportive for you and your unique needs.

Write a list of three physical movements that feel realistic and inspiring for you at this moment. Examples: Taking the stairs at work, going for a morning walk, attending a yoga class, stretching gently each morning.

1. _____

_____

_____

_____

2. _____

_____

_____

_____

3. _____

_____

_____

_____

RELEASE YOUR TENSION

You'll be surprised to feel the tension you unknowingly hold in your neck and shoulders. To release this tightness, stop where you are, and take a deep breath.

▸ Relax your shoulders down your back, and unclench your jaw.

▸ Gently roll your head three times to the right and then three times to the left. Move your head in a conscious way that allows your neck muscles to loosen with each movement. Doesn't that feel good?

Use this simple exercise anytime to create a moment of calm and address the stress you're holding.

HOW DO YOU FEEL?

Have you ever stopped to consider how working out makes you feel? Whether you work out at a gym or at home, it all counts. Sure, it's easy to skip the gym after a long day, but remembering the feeling of post-workout bliss can inspire you to keep moving.

How does completing a workout make you feel?

REPRIORITIZE IT

In our busy lives, it's easy for exercise to get knocked from our to-do list. Let's work on reprioritizing.

Write down three current blocks you have around physical movement. Examples: There's not enough time, not motivated to start, not sure what workouts to try.

Then, under each block, write an actionable statement to help you overcome it when you feel stuck. Examples: Mark it on the calendar, join with a friend, do an internet search for fun and different exercise ideas.

1. _____

_____

_____

_____

2. _____

_____

_____

_____

3. _____

_____

_____

_____

"IT'S NOT
ABOUT PERFECT. IT'S
ABOUT EFFORT. AND WHEN
YOU BRING THAT EFFORT
EVERY SINGLE DAY, THAT'S
WHERE TRANSFORMATION
HAPPENS. THAT'S HOW
CHANGE OCCURS."

—Jillian Michaels

STAIR CHALLENGE

Don't have the time or energy for an intense workout? For the next three days, simply challenge yourself to take the stairs every opportunity you get (within reason, of course!).

Begin to take notice of any changes—increased energy, improved stamina, enhanced mood—that you experience.

DEAR EXERCISE . . .

What's your relationship with physical activity? An honest assessment will paint a clearer picture of where you stand. Let this clarity help release any guilt or uneasiness you may feel and inspire you to invite movement back into your day.

Freewrite about your current relationship with exercise. If you need help, imagine that you're talking to a friend and filling them in on your status.

ENVISION YOUR SUPPORT TEAM

Having someone who can support you and hold you accountable in a new journey can make all the difference in your success. List some people who can inspire you to keep going when you lack motivation.

If you're up for it, take a step further and let one of those people know you might be calling on them for support.

BE IN NATURE

No matter where you live, challenge yourself to get out in nature for 30 minutes today. Head to a local hiking trail or your neighborhood park, as long as it's somewhere with trees and grass.

Walk for half an hour, pausing to take note of the beauty that surrounds you. Isn't it amazing how nature can heal us and make us feel connected to ourselves and the world around us?

GOALS OF THE GAME

When you start anything new, goals or intentions can make the process feel more approachable and measurable. In the two columns provided, write a list of three physical goals and three nonphysical goals you'd like to achieve through exercise. Physical goals can include less pain, more flexibility, and increased stamina. Nonphysical goals can include improved mood, more energy and better sleep.

PHYSICAL GOALS	NONPHYSICAL GOALS
1.	1.
2.	2.
2.	3.

TRY SOMETHING NEW

If exercise feels out of reach, maybe you just haven't found something that excites you yet.

Sign up for a new workout class to switch up your typical workout routine or challenge your idea of how working out should look.

If you love to spin, sign up for yoga. If you're more of a Pilates person, try a kickboxing class. Not sure where to start? Pick an exercise that sounds like something you'd enjoy, and commit to signing up for one new class this week. If you're not into group exercise, look online for a stretching, yoga, or workout video you can do right in your home.

15-MINUTE MOVE CHALLENGE

Self-care helps us realize that significant changes can occur in the small moments we create exclusively for ourselves.

For the next five days, challenge yourself to move your body for 15 minutes a day. Focus on making those small moments a priority.

Here are some ideas to get you moving: Walk to work instead of taking the bus, opt for the stairs when possible, take your dog for a stroll, park farther away in the parking lot, or toss a ball with a child or friend.

DEAR BODY, THANK YOU

Thank your body for all it does for you by filling in the blanks below.

Dear Body,

I wanted to say thank you. Thank you for all the

things you do for me, including _____,

_____, and _____.

It's true, I'm not always easy on you, but I

plan to treat you with _____ and

_____ moving forward. I promise to

_____ more often and ensure that I focus

on getting more _____ in throughout the

day.

Thank you for always being there for me.

Love,

_____
YOUR NAME HERE

GET UP AND DANCE

Pick a favorite song that inspires you to move, and then get up and do it! Challenge yourself to step outside your comfort zone and dance around like nobody's watching.

You might feel silly at first, but a solo dance party can boost your energy, harness your playful creativity, and greatly improve your mood. Notice how a little movement helps your mood shift in such a short time. After you dance it out, record how you feel on the lines below.

HYDRATE, HYDRATE, HYDRATE

All of this movement requires proper hydration. Challenge yourself to drink at least eight 8-ounce glasses of water every day. Keep a reusable bottle handy if you are on the go.

Caring for your basic physical needs is an essential part of self-care, helping you feel your best and nourish your body from the inside out.

INSPIRATION TO KEEP GOING

Think about what you'd like to hear most when things feel tough. Write three motivational sentences that will inspire you to keep moving. If you want, write these sentences in a place you often see: a sticky note on your bathroom mirror, the background of your phone, or next to your sneakers.

1. _____

_____

_____

_____

2. _____

_____

_____

_____

3. _____

_____

_____

_____

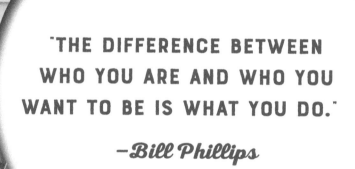

"THE DIFFERENCE BETWEEN WHO YOU ARE AND WHO YOU WANT TO BE IS WHAT YOU DO."

–Bill Phillips

LUNCHTIME POWER HOUR

It's so easy to get stuck in the habit of eating lunch at your desk in front of your computer. Today, get up and get out. Stretch your legs and spend part of your lunch break outside taking a short walk. If you can't get out, walk up a few flights of stairs and back down again. Either way, you'll receive the benefits of fresh blood flow and a midafternoon energy boost without caffeine. Feels good, huh?

VISUALIZE THE FEELING

Visualization is a powerful tool for getting crystal clear with something—a feeling, a state of being, an achievement—whatever you'd like to accomplish.

Take a moment to envision your most vibrant and healthy self, physically, emotionally, and mentally.

What are you doing? What are you saying? How are you standing? How do you feel? Who surrounds you?

Now describe yourself in detail. Embody the spirit of the "you" that you've captured in your mind and visualize stepping into that role.

A SIMPLE STRETCH

Hopefully you're just a little sore from all of this new movement. Now, reap the benefits of adding a simple stretching routine to your day.

Set a timer for five minutes and focus on gently stretching your body based on your unique needs. You can check out some stretching videos online for inspiration or just allow your body to guide you toward what feels best. This is a wonderful and peaceful way to start or end each day with self-care.

"ORGANIZATION ISN'T ABOUT PERFECTION. IT'S ABOUT EFFICIENCY, REDUCING STRESS AND CLUTTER, SAVING TIME AND MONEY, AND IMPROVING YOUR OVERALL QUALITY OF LIFE."

— *Christina Scalise*

GET ORGANIZED

or · gan · ize: to arrange into a structured whole; order

Decluttering and organizing your life, whether that means your physical space or your mind, can feel like a huge task. It may even require a strategic plan and some major motivation to just begin, much less get the job accomplished.

But consider this: The act of organization can help to relieve stress, provide feelings of calm, and deliver a satisfying sense of accomplishment. When you take the time to clean out your physical life, you're not only clearing out space in your home, you're also creating precious extra space in your busy mind. Additionally, studies show that increased clutter can impact the amount of pleasure you experience in that space—not a good thing if you live there!

The more room you create by getting rid of what no longer serves you physically or emotionally, the more gratitude you'll have for the things that remain in your life.

The process of organizing and purging clutter in your life is a powerful form of self-care.

WHAT DID IT DO FOR YOU?

Reflect on a time you thoroughly cleaned out a room in your home. You may have emptied the drawers, dusted and cleaned, and donated what you no longer used.

How did you feel after completing the task? Write it in the space provided, and as you work through the next exercises in this section, remember these positive emotions.

A MEDITATION FOR LETTING GO

As you begin getting organized, you may feel a little stressed or overwhelmed at the physical and emotional process of releasing items that no longer serve you. Meditation can help you feel more prepared and confident about your decisions.

▸ To begin, set a timer for five minutes if you wish, and sit in a quiet, relaxing space.

▸ Gently close your eyes, bringing your attention to your breath. Breathe deeply and intentionally, in through your nose and out through your mouth.

▸ As you breathe, visualize yourself releasing items that no longer have a place in your home. As you do, imagine also releasing the physical sense of stress or burden that comes with each item, and feel that burden leaving your body. Focus on the expanding feeling of empowerment and calm this process can bring.

▸ With each inhalation, silently repeat the words *I am expanding*.

▸ With each exhalation, silently repeat the words *I am releasing*.

▸ When the time is up, gently open your eyes.

Call on this meditation anytime you feel overwhelmed by the decluttering process. Keep in touch with those positive feelings that are on the other side of releasing what you no longer need.

CREATE A PLAN

Create a list of all the spaces in your home that you'd like to organize—small or large—and include whatever resources you require to get the job done, such as extra hands, storage containers, cleaning supplies, etc.

Commit to checking off one area on your list each week. Watch how your home begins to transform—and your well-being along with it.

START A DONATION "DROPBOX"

Grab an empty box or bag and create a donation dropbox in a visible corner of your home (by the front or back door works great—it symbolizes "this is going out of here").

Throughout the week, add items that don't have a place in your home or that you no longer use. As you slowly declutter and create more space, consider how your items will support those in need. It's a win-win!

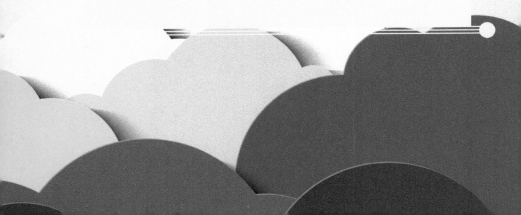

"THE BEST WAY TO
FIND OUT WHAT WE
TRULY NEED IS TO GET RID
OF WHAT WE DON'T."

—Marie Kondo

CONSIDER WHAT YOU'LL GAIN

Have you ever stopped to consider all that can be gained by getting organized? In fact, the physical, emotional, and mental benefits are endless.

Create a list of what you can anticipate gaining, such as decreased stress, more mental clarity, space to see things, and less "stuff," by clearing up the clutter in your life.

ADDRESS EMOTIONAL ATTACHMENT

As you declutter, you may find that it feels tough to let particular physical objects go. Emotional attachment to certain clothing items, family heirlooms, or special gifts is common, but if you're really feeling like your stuff is closing in on you, why not take some time to decide which items are truly worth keeping?

Use the following chart to help you navigate the feelings and anxieties that might pop up while organizing. Simply pick up an item and repeat a word out loud from each column that best describes how the item makes you feel. For example, *This sweater makes me feel happy, and it is something I cherish.*

If you come across an object that doesn't align with the chart, put it in your donation box.

The object makes me feel:	The object:
○ happy	○ is useful
○ grateful	○ is something I cherish
○ excited	○ is unique

15-MINUTE CLEANUP

For the next five days, prioritize 15 minutes each morning to dedicate to straightening up. Set a timer for 15 minutes, turn on your favorite music or podcast, and get cleaning. Whether you choose to make the bed, put away clean clothes, empty the dishwasher, or start a load of laundry, the benefits of getting a jump start on your day include feeling great!

IF YOU COULD WAVE A MAGIC WAND . . .

If you could change one thing about the current way you organize your space, what would it be? Maybe you'd like more kitchen cabinet space or less clutter in the garage? Perhaps you'd love to see more systems in place for managing monthly bills? Or maybe your self-care toiletries could use a long-overdue overhaul.

Write down one thing you want to change and three action items that you can take to help achieve that vision.

One thing I would like to change:

_____

_____

_____

_____

_____

_____

Three steps I can take to get there:

1. _____

_____

2. _____

_____

3. _____

_____

ORGANIZE THE MAIL

Are your mailbox and inbox overflowing? Commit to reducing clutter and waste by going paperless with all bills and accounts— receive email reminders instead. And instead of deleting unwanted emails, take a few moments to unsubscribe from those you no longer wish to receive. By thinning the herd of incoming mail, you'll help save time, declutter your home and your mind, and preserve your sanity.

Going forward, make it a habit to unsubscribe from five different emails every Wednesday.

YOUR PERFECT SPACE

Have you ever seen a home (in real life or in a magazine) that seemed perfectly organized and decorated? Take a moment to reflect on your current surroundings, and then take five minutes and freewrite about what you love about your space, what you dislike, what you would change, and what characteristics your organized and perfectly appointed space would have.

CHECK UP ON YOUR HEALTH

Confession time: How long has it been since your last physical exam? One of the most important things we can do for our self-care, as well as our peace of mind, is to get organized and up-to-date on all necessary health appointments.

Consider whether it's time to see the doctor, dentist, eye doctor, and gynecologist as well as to book any applicable procedures, such as a mammogram or colonoscopy. Get any questionable skin issues looked at by a dermatologist. Agreed, none of this is fun, but knowing your physical needs are attended to is a wonderful feeling.

If you're resistant to any of this, enlist a friend to do the same so you can boost each other's courage and know that you're keeping one another accountable and healthy.

Make a list below of any health-related appointments you need to make in the coming weeks.

CLOSET CLEANOUT

When was the last time you went through your clothes? Take inventory of the clothes hanging in your closet, folded in your dresser, and in storage under your bed. Put on some music or your favorite podcast and start to sort through your items.

Here's your challenge: If you haven't worn an article of clothing in more than a year, donate it to someone in need.

FIND FINANCIAL AND MENTAL CLARITY

Monthly subscription services can really add up, sometimes even without our knowledge.

Make a list of all of the subscription services you're currently paying for every month, quarter, or year, including the cost of each one. Review your credit card statements for recurring charges, dig into your app store, and think about where else subscriptions could be hiding.

Then cancel or deactivate any subscriptions that you no longer deem necessary. Add them up to see how much money you're saving simply by getting organized and rethinking your priorities. How does it make you feel to free up this space, both financially and mentally?

AFFIRMATIONS FOR CLEARING SPACE

As you declutter and organize your space, you may feel resistance to the process. To help ease this discomfort, create three encouraging affirmations in the space provided. Here is an example: *I am creating space for what I need most in life.*

When you find yourself facing a block in the organizational process, call on these affirmations to remind you of what you hope to gain from your efforts!

1. _____

_____

_____

_____

_____

2. _____

_____

_____

_____

3. _____

_____

_____

_____

_____

MESSY DRAWER, MESSY MIND

Do you know that one drawer we all have in our home? That catchall of keys, rubber bands, stamps, checks, pens, old matchbooks, and other various odds and ends. Yes, the junk drawer. Or drawers.

That drawer can result in a cluttered mind. Consider the last time you were shuffling through that drawer searching for something. Maybe you felt frustrated, angry, upset, or annoyed? It's time to change those feelings.

Today, take a deep breath and spend 10 minutes cleaning out and reorganizing this space. When finished, take a good look and reflect on the positive emotions you associate with your newly appointed space.

"BEING ORGANIZED ISN'T ABOUT GETTING RID OF EVERYTHING YOU OWN OR TRYING TO BECOME A DIFFERENT PERSON; IT'S ABOUT LIVING THE WAY YOU WANT TO LIVE, BUT BETTER."

—Andrew Mellen

A MEDITATION FOR EMBRACING CHANGE

Learning to release what we no longer require can feel tricky, but focusing on what we're welcoming in can ease the process. Use the following meditation to help encourage the cycle of releasing the old and welcoming the new.

▸ Sit in a chair with your feet flat on the ground, and set a timer for five minutes if you wish.

▸ Rest your hands with palms facing up on your legs, and gently close your eyes.

▸ Calm your mind and take three deep breaths, in through your nose and out through your mouth.

▸ Continue with your deep breathing.

▸ With each exhalation, silently repeat the words *I release*.

▸ With each inhalation, silently repeat the words *I welcome and embrace*.

▸ When the time is up, gently open your eyes and take note of how you feel.

ORGANIZE A SWAP

Instead of buying something new, organize a swap with your local friends. Encourage everyone to bring items they no longer use, such as clothing, kid and baby gear, or seasonal items, and make an afternoon of connecting and finding new treasures.

UNEXPECTED DISCOVERIES

Hopefully, you've found new ways to declutter and organize your life throughout this section—and with them, a wonderful sense of accomplishment. There are many well-known advantages to clearing out a space, such as decreased feelings of stress and being overwhelmed, increased happiness, and a sense of peace and calm.

Now, reflect on some of the unexpected benefits you may have discovered throughout this process. Perhaps you find yourself sleeping better at night, or you no longer get frustrated walking into a particular room in your home. Maybe you're more efficient, feeling more grounded, or even inspired to do more in this area.

Share three unexpected benefits you discovered.

1. _____

_____

_____

_____

_____

2. _____

_____

_____

_____

3. _____

_____

_____

_____

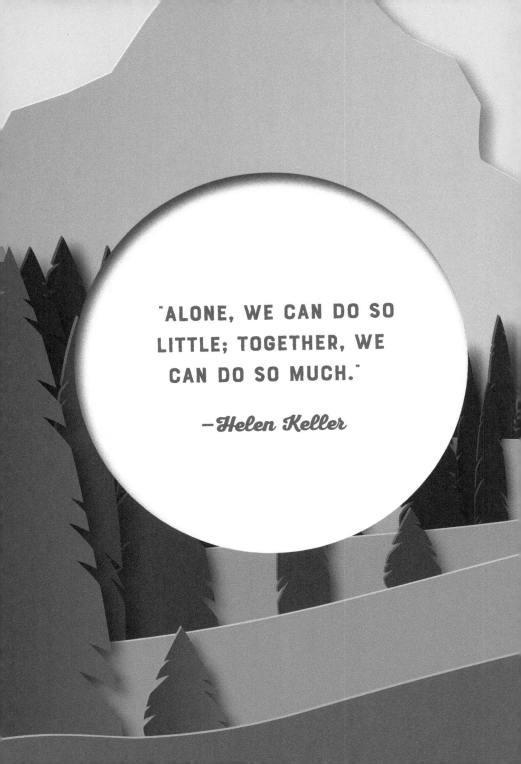

"ALONE, WE CAN DO SO LITTLE; TOGETHER, WE CAN DO SO MUCH."

—Helen Keller

Section Five

EMBRACE YOUR COMMUNITY

com · mun · i · ty: a feeling of fellowship with others, as a result of sharing common attitudes, interests, and goals

We've seen how self-care encourages you to tend to your needs and happiness. However, did you know that it also empowers you to help those around you?

When we ourselves are not feeling cared for, it can be overwhelming to serve others, whether it be family, friends, coworkers, neighbors, or our global community. As a result, we may act from a place of obligation rather than intention.

When we take the time to fill ourselves up before tending to others, we are more capable of showing up as the best possible version of ourselves. We give from a place of overflow and gratitude rather than a place of guilt. In turn, we experience a deeper level of joy by witnessing the positive impact of our actions.

The more you are able to wholeheartedly show up for others, the more deeply fulfilled you will begin to feel.

WHAT'S COMMUNITY TO YOU?

When you think of the word "community," what comes to mind? Write a few sentences that encompass your current thoughts on community in general. Then consider where you fit into that picture. What role or roles do you play?

YOUR COMMUNITY IS . . .

Think about your own community or support system. What words come to mind? Circle the best choices from the following list.

Supportive   Genuine

Loving   Compassionate

Open-minded   Distant from me

Caring   Needy

Honest   Opinionated

Integrity-filled   Judgmental

As you work through this section, keep these words in mind and consider how you can show up with the positive qualities you circled, as well as how you can improve upon any negative qualities that may exist. Use the positive traits as fuel to step out and be of service to others.

LIFT YOURSELF BY LIFTING YOUR LOCAL COMMUNITY

The smallest act can lift another. What's one little action you could take today to improve the community that surrounds you? Consider dropping off cans to a local food bank, donating to your local charity, assisting an elderly neighbor, or picking up litter.

List three charitable actions you could do to support your local community that would feel good to you.

1.

2.

3.

HOST A DINNER PARTY

Reach out to those you love and invite them to a dinner party in your home. There's something so gratifying and grounding about preparing a meal with love, serving it to those you care for most, and connecting with one another in a fun and relaxed setting.

If you're up to it, commit to a monthly dinner party and rotate hosting duties throughout the members of your group.

"WE DON'T HAVE TO DO IT ALONE. WE WERE NEVER MEANT TO."

—Brené Brown

REFLECT ON GIVING

Take a moment to reflect on the last time you performed an act of charity. Maybe you volunteered your time, money, or other resources or initiated a random act of kindness.

How did you feel at that moment? Write about the emotions you felt by being of service to others.

CONNECT WITH COMMUNITY

Put yourself out there and connect with your local community.

Sign up for a local event, take a trip to a yoga or meditation studio, or head to your local library or place of worship. These are all great spots to step outside your comfort zone and connect with your neighbors. You never know who you'll meet.

CHOOSE YOUR CAUSE

Instead of merely thinking about volunteering, get out there and do it. Create a list of three local organizations that you're interested in helping, and write a few sentences about why each cause speaks to you. Take it a step further and ask a friend to join in. Find a date that works for both of you. The sooner you get it on the calendar, the more likely it'll happen!

1. _____

_____

_____

_____

_____

2. _____

_____

_____

_____

_____

3. _____

_____

_____

_____

_____

THANK YOUR GO-TO
SUPPORT PERSON

Do you have a go-to person when it comes to asking for support or advice? This person could be a friend, a coworker, a loved one, a family member, or even your therapist.

Take a moment to write them a letter expressing your gratitude for their role in your life. Consider their qualities that make you feel comfortable opening up to them.

Dear _____,
SUPPORT PERSON

_____

_____

_____

_____

_____

_____

Love,

_____
YOUR NAME HERE

RANDOM ACTS OF KINDNESS

Challenge yourself to perform a random act of kindness each day for the next seven days. This practice doesn't have to cost you a penny. Hold the door open for someone, give a genuine compliment, smile at a stranger, or purchase coffee for the person behind you in line.

Notice the shift in your spirit after completing this act, and consider how you can integrate random acts of kindness into your daily life.

CONSIDER HOW YOU
SUPPORT OTHERS

Share three ways that you intentionally support others in your life. Maybe you have a weekly phone date with a loved one who lives far away or you offer to babysit your neighbor's kids so they can have a night off?

    If nothing comes to mind, write a few ideas of how you can begin to support those around you more intentionally and lovingly in ways that would feel good to you, too.

GO LOCAL

For the next week, try your best to avoid big-box stores and big-name online retailers and instead shop locally and support small business owners as much as possible.

Look at the bigger feel-good picture: Money spent at locally owned businesses tends to stay in the community, whereas money spent at big-box stores does not. Investing your money in local businesses helps to pay for that business owner's grocery bills, their kid's dance lessons, and more. And small businesses are part of what makes your town unique.

SET INTENTIONS FOR GIVING

Setting intentions helps create clarity around how you want to show up in the world. When it comes to your local community, how do you intend to support those around you? Creating intention behind the actions you choose to support your local community can take giving to another, more meaningful level, for both you and the receiver.

Consider the ways that you could give back to your community and back up each action with an intention. Write down three action/intention statements. For example, *I'd like to volunteer at the local soup kitchen, and I intend to inspire others to join in by sharing my experiences.*

1. _____

_____

_____

_____

2. _____

_____

_____

_____

3. _____

_____

_____

_____

THE JOY OF GIVING
WITHOUT EXPECTATION

The act of reaching out and supporting your local community can feel deeply rewarding and fulfilling. These feelings can be enhanced when we give to others without any expectation to receive something in return.

Have you ever stopped to consider where you find your joy in giving to others? Do you provide for others with the hope of receiving validation or something else in return, or are you giving selflessly?

Take a few moments to reflect on this question and freewrite in the space provided.

_____

_____

_____

_____

_____

_____

_____

_____

_____

To take this a step further, decide to pay an anonymous kindness. You might leave flowers on a neighbor's step, shovel the snow off someone's walk, or secretly deliver treats to somebody who helps you at work and then tell no one. Note how this makes you feel.

AN AFFIRMATION FOR EMBRACING COMMUNITY

For some people, it can feel challenging to ask for help. Others may have trouble knowing how to support the people around them. The following affirmation is designed to help you receive and give support to others in a way that feels empowering.

Find a quiet space with a mirror. Take a look at yourself and repeat the affirmation out loud three times:

I CAN FEEL EMPOWERED BY SUPPORTING THOSE AROUND ME, AND I AM WORTHY OF ACCEPTING THEIR SUPPORT IN RETURN.

LEARN HOW TO ASK FOR HELP

A beautiful thing happens when we reach out to those around us and ask for what we need. Our vulnerability empowers others to step up and be of service, making our sense of community stronger than before.

If you're someone who doesn't ask for help regularly, consider reaching out and asking for support. If someone asks how they can help you, be honest. Keep in mind that you're creating an opportunity for someone to feel good about themselves. Plus you'll receive the support you need!

Set a timer for five minutes if you wish, and freewrite your feelings around vulnerability and asking for support.

ASK HOW YOU CAN HELP

Create a list of three people in your life whom you'd like to support in some way. Consider your neighbors, family members, colleagues—whoever is coming through to you at this moment. Then challenge yourself to reach out to each person, ask what support they need most right now, and offer to help.

Offering support with the intent of genuinely meeting someone's needs is vastly more impactful than supporting someone with what we think they might want.

A MEDITATION FOR GRATITUDE

It's easy to forget just how many people we have supporting us in our lives. From the local bus driver to the postal delivery person to our closest family and friends—they all matter. Taking a step back and turning inward can help generate gratitude for what's around you, including the community members that you perhaps take for granted.

▸ Sit in a chair with your feet flat on the ground. Set a timer for five minutes if you wish.

▸ Rest your hands with palms facing up on your legs, and gently close your eyes.

▸ Calm your mind and take three deep breaths, in through your nose and out through your mouth.

▸ Continue with your deep breathing.

▸ With each breath, reflect on your gratitude for someone in your community. Envision their face, and focus on how they support you in their own unique way.

▸ When time is up, gently open your eyes and take note of how you feel. Do you find yourself feeling more grateful for the simple acts of support around you?

UNEXPECTED DISCOVERIES

Set a timer for ten minutes, if you wish, and take some time to reflect on your journey throughout this section. As you intentionally reached out to the people who surround you, what lessons did you learn about yourself? What did you learn about giving and receiving? What did you uncover about your community and the surprising people who resonated with you?

Share what you've discovered in the space provided.

_____

_____

_____

_____

_____

_____

_____

_____

_____

_____

_____

_____

_____

_____

_____

_____

_____

"BEGIN TO GIVE YOURSELF
THE SAME CARE AND
ATTENTION YOU GIVE TO
OTHERS AND WATCH
YOURSELF BLOOM."

—Unknown

RESOURCES .

BOOKS

Boundaries with Soul by Carley Schweet
Based on a five-step method, *Boundaries with Soul* guides readers through the process of setting soulful boundaries and discovering their loving "no." It's both relatable and easy to follow.

Present Over Perfect by Shauna Niequist
Discover the power of releasing perfection and tapping into the present moment. This book is practical, approachable, and filled with aha moments.

365 Tiny Love Challenges by Lori Deschene
Tap into your self-love daily with these simple, inspiring self-love challenges.

The Self-Love Experiment by Shannon Kaiser
This practical book includes the necessary steps to remove fear-based thoughts and encourage you to fall in love with yourself all over again.

Rising Strong by Brené Brown
The simple act of vulnerability has the power to change your life. Learning how to get back up and own your story is a critical part in creating powerful self-care, and this book will inspire you to do just that.

The Subtle Art of Not Giving a F*ck by Mark Manson
If you're looking for a book that tells it like it is, I highly recommend picking up this one. It'll help you uncover what's essential to devote energy to and what you can let go of in pursuit of the life you've always wanted to live.

WEBSITES

These websites are vast, incredible resources for those seeking to create a life rooted in holistic wellness. You'll find inspiration, thought-provoking insights, and more.

Holistic Self-Care Blog
www.carleyschweet.com

Tiny Buddha
www.tinybuddha.com

mindbodygreen
www.mindbodygreen.com

Well + Good
www.wellandgood.com

Find a Therapist in Your Area
www.psychologytoday.com/us

INSPIRING INSTAGRAM ACCOUNTS

The following Instagram accounts are ones I love to follow and be inspired by daily. They are thought-provoking, encourage holistic self-care, and empower their followers to live a life that feels both brave and filled with happiness.

@therapyuntangled by Stephanie Essenfeld

@alex_elle by Alex Elle

@notesfromyourtherapist by Allyson Dinneen

@lizandmollie by Liz and Mollie

@selfcareisforeveryone a self-care community

REFERENCES

Godman, Heidi. "Regular Exercise Changes the Brain to Improve Memory, Thinking Skills." *Harvard Health Blog*. Last modified April 5, 2018. http://www.health.harvard.edu/blog/regular-exercise -changes-brain-improve-memory-thinking-skills-201404097110.

Gregoire, Carolyn. "Why Finding Time for Creativity Each Day Makes You Happier." *Huffington Post*. December 2, 2016. http:// www.huffpost.com/entry/creativity-happiness-psychology _n_58419e0ce4b0c68e0480689a.

Lexico Online Dictionary. "Community." Accessed December 17, 2019. http://www.lexico.com/en/definition/community.

Lexico Online Dictionary. "Creativity." Accessed December 2, 2019. http://www.lexico.com/en/definition/creativity.

Lexico Online Dictionary. "Movement." Accessed December 5, 2019. http://www.lexico.com/en/definition/movement.

Lexico Online Dictionary. "Nurture." Accessed November 15, 2019. http://www.lexico.com/en/definition/nurture.

Lexico Online Dictionary. "Organize." Accessed December 16, 2019. http://www.lexico.com/en/definition/organize.

Merriam-Webster Online Dictionary. "Expand." Accessed November 26, 2019. http://www.merriam-webster.com /dictionary/expand.

Whitbourne, Susan Krauss. "5 Reasons to Clear the Clutter Out of Your Life." *Psychology Today*. May 13, 2017. http://www.psychologytoday.com/us/blog/fulfillment-any-age/201705/5-reasons-clear-the-clutter-out-your-life.

ACKNOWLEDGMENTS

This journal wouldn't have come to life without the support of my husband, Corbin Nakamura. At the time of writing, I was in my final weeks of pregnancy, secretly working on this book, and determined to pour everything I could into making this journal a reality. From walking the dogs to bringing me breakfast to refilling my mug of tea, your support made this journal possible. Thank you.

Also, a *huge* thank you to my online business manager Chynna Benton and the Byte Bodega team. I would be lost without your impeccable organization skills and keen ability to spot problems before they exist. Thank you for supporting my work so passionately.

To my parents, thank you doesn't even begin to express how deeply grateful I am to have the two of you in my life as my guides. Your unwavering support is appreciated more than you know, and this journal wouldn't be possible without either of you.

Lastly, a deep heartfelt thank you to the Callisto Media team, especially Emily Angell and Susan Haynes. Thank you both for your patience and guidance and for entrusting me to create this journal to support others on their self-care journey.

ABOUT THE AUTHOR

Carley Schweet is a holistic self-care coach and author of the book and digital course *Boundaries with Soul*.

After years of people-pleasing in the corporate fashion industry in New York City, she finally realized there was more to life than being a chronic yes-woman. By practicing transformational self-care and discovering her loving No, she gained more confidence and discovered that by making her needs a priority, true happiness would soon follow.

Carley is the host of the *You Time* podcast, and her work is featured on major media outlets such as *FabFitFun*, *MindBodyGreen*, *Bustle*, *Hello Giggles*, and *Elite Daily*.

You can connect with Carley on Instagram at ***@carley_schweet*** and discover more about creating holistic self-care practices at carleyschweet.com.

CPSIA information can be obtained
at www.ICGtesting.com
Printed in the USA
LVHW020342270320
651340LV00003B/3